Children's Authors

C.S. Lewis

Jill C. Wheeler
ABDO Publishing Company

visit us at
www.abdopublishing.com

Published by ABDO Publishing Company, 8000 West 78th Street, Edina, Minnesota 55439.
Copyright © 2009 by Abdo Consulting Group, Inc. International copyrights reserved in all
countries. No part of this book may be reproduced in any form without written permission from the
publisher. The Checkerboard Library™ is a trademark and logo of ABDO Publishing Company.

Printed in the United States.

Cover Photo: Getty Images
Interior Photos: Alamy p. 19; Corbis p. 13; Getty Images pp. 5, 17, 18; Photograph Courtesy of
    University of Dundee Archive Services p. 21; Used by permission of The Marion E. Wade
    Center, Wheaton College, Wheaton, IL pp. 6, 7, 9, 11, 15

Editors: Tamara L. Britton, Megan M. Gunderson
Art Direction: Neil Klinepier

Library of Congress Cataloging-in-Publication Data

Wheeler, Jill C., 1964-
  C.S. Lewis / Jill C. Wheeler.
     p. cm. -- (Children's authors)
  Includes bibliographical references and index.
  ISBN 978-1-60453-077-3
  1. Lewis, C. S. (Clive Staples), 1898-1963--Juvenile literature. 2. Authors, English--20th century-
-Biography--Juvenile literature. I. Title.

  PR6023.E926Z953 2009
  823'.912--dc22
  [B]
                                    2008004802

Contents

Welcome to Narnia

In 2005, millions of people flocked to movie theaters to see a new fantasy film. *The Chronicles of Narnia: The Lion, the Witch and the **Wardrobe*** was a **box office** hit. It also introduced many people to an amazing author. His name is C.S. Lewis.

For more than 35 years, Lewis taught at Oxford and Cambridge universities in England. There, he wrote many books about Christianity and Christian faith. He was also a successful author of children's fantasy novels.

Lewis never set out to become a writer for children. He simply wrote about subjects that interested him, such as myths and animals. It just happened that these topics also interested kids!

Since 1950, readers have bought 95 million books from The Chronicles of Narnia series. It was the world's best-selling children's fantasy series for many years. Today, only J.K. Rowling's Harry Potter series has sold more books than The Chronicles of Narnia series!

C.S. Lewis

Seashore Summers

Clive Staples Lewis was born on November 29, 1898, in Belfast, Ireland. His father, Albert, was a **solicitor**. His mother, Florence, was a talented mathematician. Clive had an older brother named Warren, who was called Warnie. When he was just four years old, Clive asked to be called Jacksie. This was eventually shortened to Jack.

Jack's family was like most middle-class households of that time. Florence stayed home to manage the house. There was a cook, a maid, a gardener, and a **governess**. Jack and Warnie did not attend

Florence Lewis

school. Instead, they were taught at home.

When Jack was a toddler, the family spent summers at the seashore. Florence, Jack, Warnie, and the **governess** took a train to their rented housing. Albert stayed in Belfast to work. He sometimes visited them on weekends.

Albert Lewis

At the seashore, Jack and Warnie played games. They also fished and swam in the ocean. Jack never forgot those summer vacations. He developed a lifelong love of swimming as a result of his time by the sea.

Little Lea

In 1905, the Lewises had a house built for them. They named it Little Lea. It was a three-story brick home with many hideaways, nooks, and crannies. The house had long passages, creaky attics, and gurgling pipes! It provided plenty of inspiration for Jack's imagination.

Jack and his brother had a playroom. They called it the Little End Room. There, they often amused themselves by writing stories and drawing pictures. Jack created an imaginary land called Boxen. Boxen was **inhabited** by talking animals who wore clothes!

Besides writing stories, Jack also loved to read and tell them. His cousin Ruth recalled how she, Jack, and Warnie would crawl into a large **wardrobe**. There, they would sit in the dark and listen as Jack told stories.

Jack's stories were always full of details. Sometimes they had scary characters. Jack later said that even his dreams were filled with frightening things such as giant bugs!

Jack (left) *and Warnie* (right)

Unfortunately, sadness soon came to Little Lea. When Jack was just nine years old, his mother learned she had **cancer**. Doctors performed surgery on Florence to try to save her life. But she died on August 23, 1908.

Off to School

Jack was devastated by his mother's death. Then, in September 1908 he had to leave home to attend boarding school. Wynyard was a school north of London, England. Warnie had studied there for three years.

Wynyard was a terrible school. Its **curriculum** was limited. The food was bad, and the school was dirty. Worst of all, the students were treated poorly. Jack was glad when the school closed for good in 1910.

The next year, Jack attended Cherbourg Preparatory School in Great Malvern, England. It was close to Malvern College, where Warnie was studying. That meant the brothers could travel to and from home together.

At Cherbourg, Jack continued writing and illustrating Boxen stories. He also began exploring northern European **mythology**. Most important, Jack excelled in his studies. In 1913, he won a **scholarship** to Malvern College.

Warnie had enjoyed Malvern College. But Jack had a different experience. The older boys often picked on him. They made him do chores, such as shining shoes. Jack was often tired and unhappy. He begged his father to let him leave Malvern. Albert finally agreed that Jack could leave in 1914.

Warnie (left), Albert, and Jack (right)

Quiet Study

Albert decided to send Jack to study with a private **tutor**. In September 1914, Jack left home to study with William T. Kirkpatrick. Kirkpatrick lived in Great Bookham, England. He had been one of Albert's teachers. He had tutored Warnie, too.

For two and a half years, Jack lived and studied with Kirkpatrick. Kirkpatrick was a tough teacher. Yet Jack learned critical thinking skills that served him well throughout his life.

Jack spent part of each day with Kirkpatrick studying classical literature and languages. The rest of the day he spent reading, writing poetry, and doing schoolwork. Kirkpatrick also worked to teach him mathematics, but Jack struggled with the subject.

While he lived in Great Bookham, Jack wrote many letters to his family and friends. He wrote to one friend that his dream was to become a poet. Meanwhile, Jack's father and his tutor decided that he would do well as an **academic**. So, Kirkpatrick prepared Jack to attend the University of Oxford.

Jack took the Oxford **scholarship** examination in December 1916. He passed the test and was offered a scholarship at University College. However, he spent just one term at Oxford before war interrupted his plans.

The University of Oxford is the oldest university in the English-speaking world.

Off to War

World War I had started in 1914. Because he was Irish, Lewis did not have to fight in the war. But when he turned 18 years old, he registered for service.

Lewis attended the officer training program at Keble College in Oxford. His roommate there was Paddy Moore. Lewis and Moore became good friends.

In November 1917, Lewis and his fellow soldiers were sent to battle in France. Lewis wrote letters to his father describing what it was like to fight in the trenches. He also managed to find time to read books and poetry.

On April 15, 1918, Lewis took part in the Battle of Arras. He was wounded when a shell exploded nearby. Lewis returned to England, where he recovered from his injury. But his friend Moore was killed in action.

Lewis and Moore had made a promise before going to war. Each pledged to take care of the other's family if one of them did not survive. Lewis kept his promise. He cared for Mrs. Moore and Paddy's sister, Maureen, for as long as they needed him.

Lewis (left), Paddy Moore (right), and friends enjoy a boat ride.

Teaching and Writing

In January 1919, Lewis returned to the University of Oxford. That September, his first book of poems was published. It is called *Spirits in Bondage*. Lewis used the **pseudonym** Clive Hamilton.

At Oxford, Lewis excelled in his studies. He wanted to earn a teaching position. In May 1925, he was offered a **fellowship** in English at Oxford's Magdalen College.

Lewis's teaching schedule allowed him time to write. He gathered each week with a group of friends to discuss writing and ideas. The group, called The Inklings, included J.R.R. Tolkien. Tolkien would become the famous author of *The Hobbit* and *The Lord of the Rings*.

Lewis and Tolkien often discussed matters of faith. As a young man, Lewis had decided he did not believe in God. But as an adult, he changed his mind. He began to write books about Christian faith and became a popular speaker on the subject.

Lewis's first book about faith is *Pilgrim's Regress*. It was published in 1933. In 1941, Lewis began giving radio broadcasts on religious topics. His book *Mere Christianity* is based on many of those radio messages.

In 1942, *The Screwtape Letters* was published. In it, two demons work to lead a man away from God. It is one of Lewis's most popular books.

Meanwhile, Lewis used his imagination to write a science fiction series. *Out of the Silent Planet* was published in 1938. *Perelandra* followed in 1943. In 1946, *That Hideous Strength* completed what became known as the Ransom Trilogy.

Lewis was featured on the cover of the September 8, 1947, issue of Time *magazine*.

Narnia

When **World War II** began, Lewis lived in a country home called The Kilns. Lewis had bought the house with Warren and Mrs. Moore. Maureen lived there, too.

During the war, Germany frequently bombed London. To keep children safe, they were sent to live in the country. Several children stayed at The Kilns.

At this time, Lewis began writing a story. In it, four brothers and sisters move to the English countryside to escape the bombing. There, behind a large **wardrobe**, they discover a magical world controlled by an evil witch.

The story became *The Lion, the Witch and the Wardrobe.* The tale of

The Chronicles of Narnia series has been translated into 41 languages.

Peter, Susan, Edmund, and Lucy Pevensie was the first of seven books about the magical land of Narnia. Lewis followed it with one Narnia book each year for the next six years.

In 2005, The Lion, the Witch and the Wardrobe was made into a movie.

Many fans begged Lewis to write more books about Narnia. He never added to the series. However, it became the world's best-selling fantasy series for children.

The Chronicles of Narnia let Lewis work with many of the topics that most interested him. The books feature a number of Christian ideas. They also draw material from Greek and Roman **mythology**. In addition, they also reflect Lewis's love of talking animals and his interest in good versus evil.

Joy

Because of his success, Lewis gained fans worldwide. One fan was American writer and poet Joy Davidman Gresham. Gresham began writing to Lewis to discuss religious questions. They shared a love of language and **debating** important issues.

Gresham and her two sons moved from New York City, New York, to London in 1953. There, Gresham and Lewis continued their friendship. Her sons, David and Douglas, also became Lewis's friends. The next year, Lewis left Oxford. He became a professor at the University of Cambridge.

In 1956, Gresham's permit to live in England **expired**. She and Lewis married in a civil ceremony so she could stay in the country. That October, Gresham learned she had **cancer**. She and her children moved to The Kilns.

Lewis and Gresham married in a Christian ceremony on March 21, 1957. Lewis was devastated when Gresham died in 1960.

Lewis was in poor health when his wife died. He resigned from Cambridge in 1963 due to illness. C.S. Lewis died of heart failure on November 22, 1963.

The Kilns is now open to the public. Fans can also see the **wardrobe** in which Lewis used to tell stories. It is at Wheaton College in Wheaton, Illinois.

Lewis's works remain popular. In 2008, a movie version of his book *The Chronicles of Narnia: Prince Caspian* was released. To this day, C.S. Lewis continues to delight!

Lewis and Gresham at The Kilns. The 1994 movie Shadowlands *is based on their relationship.*

Glossary

academic - a member of an institution of learning.

box office - income from ticket sales of a movie or a play. Also, a booth or an office where tickets for a movie or a play are sold.

cancer - any of a group of often deadly diseases characterized by an abnormal growth of cells that destroys healthy tissues and organs.

curriculum - the courses offered by an educational institution.

debate - to discuss a question or a topic, often publicly.

expire - to come to an end.

fellowship - a position given to a college or university student that allows him or her to continue studies.

governess - a person who cares for and supervises children at home.

inhabit - to live in or occupy a region.

mythology - a collection of myths from a certain group of people.

pseudonym (SOO-duh-nihm) - a fictitious name, often used by an author.

scholarship - a gift of money to help a student pay for instruction.

solicitor - a British lawyer who represents people in lower courts.

tutor - to teach a student privately. The teacher is also called a tutor.

wardrobe - a large trunk in which clothes may be hung.

World War I - from 1914 to 1918, fought in Europe. Great Britain, France, Russia, the United States, and their allies were on one side. Germany, Austria-Hungary, and their allies were on the other side.

World War II - from 1939 to 1945, fought in Europe, Asia, and Africa. Great Britain, France, the United States, the Soviet Union, and their allies were on one side. Germany, Italy, Japan, and their allies were on the other side.

Web Sites

To learn more about C.S. Lewis, visit ABDO Publishing Company on the World Wide Web at **www.abdopublishing.com**. Web sites about C.S. Lewis are featured on our Book Links page. These links are routinely monitored and updated to provide the most current information available.

Index